GIZMO

Goes to a
Baseball Game

Copyright © 2025 Heidi Heisel

All rights reserved. No part of this publication may be reproduced, distributed or transmitted in any form or by any means, including photocopying, recording, or other electronic or mechanical methods, without the prior written permission of the author.

eBook Designed by

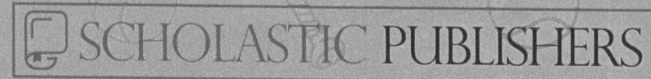

Dedication

This book is dedicated to the failures who keep on trying.

I found Gizmo on the freeway. A little white ball of fur about to merge with traffic.

One slam of the brakes and both of our lives changed forever.

The day was here
it had finally come.
Gizmo's first baseball game,
it was going to be so fun.

There was one thing
he wanted to do,
to meet his idol Chico,
the team's mascot, a little dog too.

Chico's picture
hung over his bed.
An awesome Chihuahua,
dressed in baseball red.

Excitement and energy
danced in the air.
Good cheer and good food,
baseball fans were everywhere.

But slumped in a corner,
Gizmo couldn't help but see,
a little boy crying,
his head tucked in his knees.

The game was about to start,
but that mattered none.
It was more important to be nice,
than to watch a few home runs.

Gizmo climbed on his lap,
he was sad and all alone.
His dad was supposed to meet him,
but he got stuck on the phone.

One inning turned into eight,
as the two just quietly sat.
Eating popcorn and peanuts,
to the distant sound of the bat.

Finally the dad showed up,
as the ninth was about to begin.
Gizmo found his seat,
just in time to watch the home team win.

Gizmo looked for Chico,
but he was nowhere to be found.
His idol had left the field,
and the crowd dwindled down.

Then all of a sudden,
Gizmo heard his name.
It was the little boy,
the one who made him miss the game.

"There's someone here I want you to meet
and he wants to meet you too.
I told him what you did for me,
when I was sad and feeling blue."

Gizmo couldn't believe his eyes,
as Chico took the field.
He was walking straight towards him,
Gizmo lost his cool and squealed.

The little boy giggled,
and Chico did too.
Gizmo couldn't believe it,
his dream had come true.

Gizmo thanked the little boy,
who was no longer in a corner.
And of course his dad,
the busy baseball team owner.

" I'm glad you're here,
to celebrate our winning.
We never lose,
we just run out of innings.

Winners are just losers,
who don't give up.
The more they fall,
the more they stand up.

We celebrate the effort,
no matter the final score.
And congratulate the winner.
No one likes a loser who's sore.

Winners keep on practicing.
It's what makes them strong.
They don't practice till they get it right,
but till they can't get it wrong.

Even when you do your best,
things won't always go your way.
You'll miss the catch,
or warm the bench all day.

There is no crying in baseball,
he winked at his son.
Be a good sport,
choose to have fun.

Just like our Mascot Chico,
who tried out for the team,
he wasn't quite skilled enough,
but he gave it his everything.

He isn't a pitcher,
like he dreamed he would be.
Now he makes dreams come true.
Our most popular MVP.

Life will throw you curve balls,
and that's ok.
Just keep on swinging,
and don't forget to play."

Written By Heidi Heisel

Heidi found Gizmo on I-10 in El Paso, Texas. Gizmo and Heidi have been traveling together ever since. The Gizmo Goes Books are the adventures from Gizmo's perspective. All of the books are written in rhyme, brought to life with River's illustrations, and the real pictures from the real adventure are included. Gizmo Goes to a Baseball Game was originally written in 2014 after an exciting game at Southwest University Park where Gizmo was thrilled to meet Chico.

Illustrated By River Wilson

River was 10 years old when we went to the game and he illustrated our first book, Gizmo Goes to a Baseball Game. He is 21 today.

For this relaunch, River re-illustrated all of the pages, but we included the originals too.

River has always been a creator. He is an artist, designer, athlete, and entrepreneur. He continues to dedicate his talent and artistic skills to help bring the amazing and inspiring adventures of Gizmo to life. He is currently a student at the University of North Texas majoring in Marketing.

www.ingramcontent.com/pod-product-compliance
Lightning Source LLC
Chambersburg PA
CBHW042054050526
44107CB00109B/1138